EALING IN THE 1930s & '40s

Old photographs of London Borough of Ealing

Compiled and annotated on behalf of

London Borough of Ealing Library Service

by

M. Gooding B.A., A.L.A.

Local History Librarian

Published by Hendon Publishing Co. Ltd., Hendon Mill, Nelson, Lancashire
Text © London Borough of Ealing Library Service, 1985
Printed by Fretwell & Cox Ltd., Healey Works, Goulbourne Street, Keighley, West Yorkshire

Introduction

THIS fourth volume of photographs selected from the London Borough of Ealing Local History Collection covers an important and eventful period in the development of the borough.

In terms of building development Acton was perhaps least affected, for its growth had been spectacular in the late nineteenth century. However, the cutting of the Western Avenue (1927–1930) brought many large industrial estates to the area.

Southall had grown slowly during the nineteenth century, but the creation of the Urban District Council in 1894 signalled a dramatic increase in the population. Nevertheless, it was not until 1936 that Southall received its Charter of Incorporation and the great spread of urban building to the north of Uxbridge Road dates from the 1930s.

Almost all of the northern part of the Borough of Ealing can trace its development to the same period. Hanwell had already developed as a dormitory area by the time of its incorporation with Ealing in 1926 although the 1930s did see the development for housing of the Cuckoo Estate.

Greenford, Perivale and West Twyford, which also joined with Ealing in 1926, were still rural areas. The cutting of the Western Avenue through Perivale during 1929 and 1930 meant the parish was quickly adopted as a site for industrial expansion and between 1931 and 1939 the area banded by Western Avenue, Horsenden Lane and the Paddington Canal was almost entirely covered by factories and houses. One event which took place in the 1930s not recorded elsewhere in this book was the transfer of West Twyford to the Borough of Willesden as a result of a boundary change in 1934. The residents of the area were, however, so violently opposed to the transfer that West Twyford was returned to Ealing in 1937.

Northolt too was little more than a village when it joined with Ealing in 1928. By 1931 the effects of the sale of manorial land were being felt as speculative builders moved in and development accelerated in the pre-war years.

Little if any development was possible in the borough during the war years. The impact of the war upon the borough was gradual and, as this book shows, preparations for meeting it were on the whole well advanced with air raid precautions being the main consideration. Many parts of the borough suffered heavy bombing, the first incident being in September 1940 when several bombs fell in Acton.

After the war, development of the remaining areas of the borough went ahead, perhaps the most important being the development for housing of the Northolt Racecourse land. This began in 1946 and was responsible for the main population increase in Northolt. Since then its development as a dormitory area has continued steadily.

I should like to express my thanks to my sister Freda, K.L.M. Gwynn, C.H. Keene, R.N.G. Rowland and Ann Terre for their assistance, and to Julie Kirby for the typing of the text.

Nancy Mandelstam has once again provided much valuable help with the research and selection of photographs for which I am most grateful.

The continued help of members of the public who possess photographs of interest and are willing either to donate or lend them to the London Borough of Ealing Library Service in order that the collection may be expanded would be much appreciated.

M. Gooding
Local History Librarian

1.   The Y.W.C.A. centre in East Acton Lane was the first in Outer London and was built on land given by the Goldsmiths' Company. H.R.H. The Duchess of York, now the Queen Mother, is seen here laying the foundation stone on 11th December 1929. She was greeted by Alderman R. T. Mence, Mayor of Acton, and the 'Cuckoo Band', from the Central London District School in Hanwell, provided a brief musical welcome. The official opening by the Lady Mayoress of London, Lady Neal, took place some months later on 26th March 1931. She was accompanied by her husband, Sir W. P. Neal, and the local newspaper claimed this was the first official visit to Acton of a Lord and Lady Mayoress of London since the City's welcome at Acton of Oliver Cromwell after the battle of Worcester in 1651.

2. Ever since it was opened in May 1901 Walpole Park has been popular with the people of Ealing and children have always enjoyed sailing their boats on the lake, as this 1930s view shows. This lake was excavated during the early part of 1905, by gangs of twenty five men, as part of the Council's efforts to cope with the unemployment problem of that time. It was hoped that, as an added attraction, the pond would also provide a fine stretch of water for skating in the winter.

3. It is hard to equate this tranquil scene *c.*1930 with today's busy junction on the Western Avenue. Horsenden Lane South was still little more than a country lane although industry had already come to the area. The buildings on the right are part of Sanderson's factory which opened in October 1929. In 1972 machine printing transferred to Hampshire and only hand printing is still carried on at Perivale. The water tower, which is such a landmark in this photograph, was demolished in 1978.

4.   Ealing Golf Club was formed in 1898, and at that time the first tee was just across the road from the club house in Kent Gardens. In 1923 a new company was formed and the freehold of the course was purchased. The whole course was drained and new greens, tees and fairways were laid out. The inaugural luncheon for the new club house in April 1930 was attended by a large number of guests (seen here outside the club house). These included the Mayor of Ealing, Alderman H. J. Baker, golfing members of Ealing Town Council, officials from neighbouring golf clubs and the Rector of Perivale, Revd A. H. M. Hope.

5. A view of Barons Pond nearly sixty years ago. The pond is opposite the gates to Gunnersbury Park which was owned by the Rothschild family from 1835 to 1925, and the name, with that of Lionel Road, reminds us of Lionel Rothschild, a baron of the Austrian Empire. The road to the right of the pond is now known as Gunnersbury Drive but before the new road was cut in the early 1930s it formed the southern part of Gunnersbury Avenue. The creeper-covered house, The Cottage, still remains, but the wall on the extreme right which once skirted the grounds of the large house known as Manor House has been demolished and the land developed for housing.

6. The forerunner of St. Stephens Orchestra was Drayton Court Amateur Band which was formed in about 1906. In February 1928 Revd L. W. Hart, Curate of St. Stephens, suggested the formation of an orchestra 'to cheer up the parish', and in May of that year the St. Stephens Dramatic and Orchestral Society was formed. The orchestra is seen here, in June 1930, playing at the church garden fête, which was held in the grounds of The Grange, St. Stephens Road. Their conductor from 1929 to 1932 was Mr H. H. Jefferies and the orchestra, which was fifteen strong, also played for morning and evening services. With the outbreak of the Second World War falling numbers caused the orchestra to be disbanded.

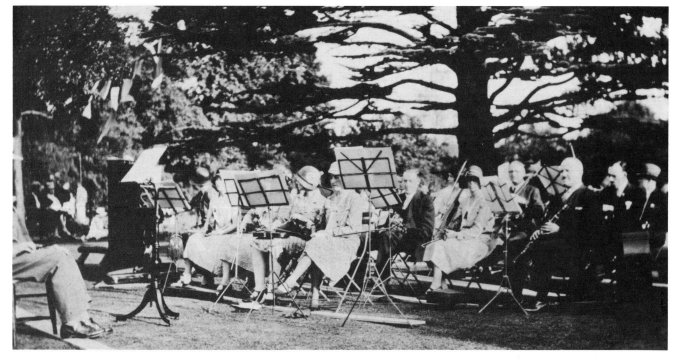

7.   Ealing Tenants Ltd was formed in 1901, and by September of that year the first nine houses were being roofed. The Brentham Estate was planned as a whole unit with a social centre, and amenities were many and varied. The Brentham Club was the focal point on the estate with regular dances, whist drives, concerts and lectures. The present Institute was opened by the Duke and Duchess of Connaught in 1911. Gardens were considered an important factor in life on the estate, and this view, taken in the early 1930s in Denison Road, shows the Brentham Horticultural Society preparing for an outing. Like many roads on the estate Denison Road was named after one of the people associated with the copartnership movement — others include Brunner, Ludlow, Neville and Holyoake.

8.   This view of Down Barns Farm in the 1930s shows haymaking time. The track lying between the haycocks and the ruined barn is Sharvel Lane, earlier Golden Bridge Lane. This was an ancient trackway leading from Harrow Hill to Uxbridge and the West, no doubt used by Saxons making their way to the pagan Saxon site of worship on the top of Harrow Hill. In the late fourteenth century the farm was owned by Sir Nicholas Brembre, who was executed for treason in 1388. It is known that nearly six hundred years before this photograph was taken wheat, oats and barley were being grown and harvested on the slopes of Down. In the late nineteenth and early twentieth centuries it was a sportsman's paradise, abounding in partridge and hare and, at one time, the then owner, Lord Hillingdon, used to entertain King Edward VII at shooting parties over Down Manor land.

9.   According to the contemporary newspaper accounts heavy showers of rain and hail had lessened the attendance at the opening of the Wesley Playing Fields in North Acton on 18th April 1931. The weather does not seem to have deterred these youngsters, however, who are obviously enjoying playing in the mud. Mr Harold Wesley, managing director of Harold Wesley Ltd, manufacturing stationers, donated two acres of land for the playing fields, Acton Council purchased another two and Middlesex County Council and others contributed to the cost of purchase and layout. The Mayor of Acton, Councillor H. Holmes, performed the opening ceremony, and in appreciation of Mr Wesley's generosity the grounds were named after him. The macebearer is Mr Arthur Labrum, who served the local authority for over forty-four years, and has a road in East Acton named after him.

10.   A splendid line-up of fire appliances photographed in 1931 at the Ealing Central Fire Station in Longfield Avenue. This fire station was built in 1888 and enlarged during 1900 and 1901. The present station on the Uxbridge Road was opened in October 1933. Shown in the picture from left to right are: Merryweather Pump Escape, Dennis Pump, Merryweather Pump and Dennis Pump Escape. Chief Officer Blakey is standing on the extreme right.

(Photo: Akers)

11.   A view of Haven Green Parade *c.*1931, before the introduction of the present one way traffic system. The
District Railway Station was opened on 1st July 1879, but the station building, seen on the right in this photograph,
was built *c.*1910. Shops were incorporated on either side of the station entrance and the building still remains,
although now converted entirely into shops since the present station was erected in the 1960s.

12.   This quiet country lane is Wood End Lane, Northolt, pictured in 1931 just prior to the development of the area. Wood End Green Farm which lay just to the north of the lane had already been sold for housing development in the 1920s. It was one of the oldest farms in Northolt and its history can be traced back to before 1244. At one time it belonged to Sir William Henry Perkin, of aniline dye fame, who sold it in November 1907. No trace of the farm remains now, the site having been built over by Reading Road and Whitton Avenue.

13.   This photograph records an event which must be almost unique in local government history. Nine oak trees were planted on St. George's Day 1931 in pairs opposite each other on the broad path leading eastward from the central bandstand in Acton Park. These, together with one planted the previous year by the then Mayor of Acton, Alderman R. T. Mence, represented one tree for each of the ten mayoral years since the incorporation of the Borough of Acton. The planting was done by the Mayor, Councillor H. Holmes, seven ex-mayors and Mrs F. A. Baldwin, the widow of the first and Charter Mayor.

14. As this picture shows, Northfield Avenue had changed considerably during the thirty years since the 1903 view reproduced in *Ealing As It Was* (plate 46). This photograph was taken a little further south and much development had taken place in the area. Northfields Station had been built in 1908, and the Avenue Theatre on the right opened in September 1932. A relatively small cinema by Cecil Massey, it became generally known as 'Spanish City' because of the elaborately decorated Moorish interior. From 1936 it was known as the Odeon, but its future today is uncertain.

15. This happy group shows Mr & Mrs Fred Croxon flanked on either side by their daughters after whom the Seven Sisters Riding School was named. Reading from left to right are Deila, Lorna, Freda, Fred Croxon, Linda, Mrs Croxon, Ida, Brenda and Stella. In 1933, when this photograph was taken, the riding school was at Medlar Farm, Northolt. The farm was situated almost at the crossroads opposite the White Hart and, like most farms, had several names during its history. In 1891 it was known as West End Farm and was let to Thomas Cotching. Mr Cotching was connected to the Ealing dairy farmers of that name and it is thought that Scotch Common, Ealing could be a corruption of Cotchings, for the family once owned the land and grazed their dairy cattle on it. In 1893 the farm was bought by T.R. Hunt and was known as Hunts Farm. By 1938 the farmhouse had been demolished and the farm was sold for development. The orchard which lay due east of the farmyard had disappeared, as had the medlar which gave the farm its last known name.

16. Although pictured at Greenford Green this is in fact the Pinner Draghounds whose First Whip was Miss Nancy Blackwell (of Crosse & Blackwell). This meeting in Autumn 1933 was the last at Greenford Green and was held there so that Mr Alfred William Perkin would be able to see, from his room, the hunt move off. Mr Perkin, son of Sir William, first followed the hounds in Greenford in 1883 with a small party of friends. The Greenford Drag Hunt grew from this, and under his mastership it became one of influence and importance, always respectful of the interests of the farmers. In November 1908 Mr Perkin celebrated his twenty-fifth year as Master of the hunt, but the First World War cut short the hunt's activities and it was never revived.

17 & 18.   Northolt Race-course opened in 1929, and these two views show the stand and enclosure in 1934, which was the year in which Northolt introduced an important innovation to British racing. This innovation was the very large electric timing clock which started up on the release of any gate from which a horse ran and was stopped by the nose of the winning horse breaking a ray across the winning line. It was a unique timing system in British racing and was not used on any other race-course until 1948. Racing ceased at Northolt in June 1940, and the course was taken over by the army ordnance depot. It later became a prisoner of war camp, and after the war the course was bought by Ealing Council. The stands were demolished in 1950 and the site developed, many of the streets being named after race-courses.

19.   J. W. Hearne's sports shop 'M.C.C. House', 137 Uxbridge Road, West Ealing was quite a landmark locally with the outsize cricket bats, balls, and stumps displayed outside. The business was started in 1852 by Tom Hearne, the first of an illustrious line of cricketers. Our photograph was taken in 1934 and shows J. W. Hearne, on the left, with Mr Flick. The shop front was damaged during the Second World War, but replaced. The business finally closed in about 1973.

20.   F. H. Rowse's drapery store was well established by the time this photograph was taken in c.1935. He had started his business in West Ealing in 1913 and the premises shown here were built in 1928, at about the same time as J. Lyons opened their shop nearby. Dolcis were newcomers, first appearing in the directories in 1934. Lyons closed in the mid-1960s, but Rowse's continued until 1982. Traffic seems to have been somewhat lighter in the 1930s, but the crush of shoppers appears to have been as great.

21.   The Silver Jubilee in May 1935 was an excuse for much celebration and festivities in the area as the following photographs show. This cheerful scene was in St. Matthews Road, Ealing, where the residents had decked their houses with flags and bunting in common with many streets and shops throughout the borough.

22. Even the taxi drivers entered into the spirit of things and decorated the cab rank at Haven Green with flags and photographs of the King and Queen.

23.　The celebrations began in earnest on Monday, 6th May 1935 when 4,000 schoolchildren took part in a pageant of history, *Events contributing to our Present Civilisation,* in thirteen scenes. The procession started at Greenford and passed through Hanwell and Ealing, finishing at Walpole Park with a festival of community singing, dancing and physical drill. This photograph was taken from the Railway Hotel, which stood on the site now occupied by Lilley & Skinner. The procession is seen turning into High Street with Sayers building on the left. Bentalls acquired the store from Sayers in 1950 and remained there until 1984 when they moved into the Ealing Broadway Centre.

24.   On the evening of 6th May 1935 there was a comic football match on Ealing Common, followed by a scout tattoo, fireworks display and what the newspaper describes as 'a glorious celebration bonfire'. The burning of the bonfire formed the end of a perfect day and provided a memorable spectacle. Some idea of its size can be seen from this photograph.

25. On Tuesday, 7th May 1935 five hundred old people were given a Jubilee Supper at the A.T.P. Film Studios on Ealing Green. The Mayor, Councillor E. H. Brooks, presided and he is seen here with the Mayoress and some of the guests. The oldest person invited was a ninety-six year-old lady, who is reported to have enjoyed both the supper and the police concert party that followed.

26 & 27.　During the week's celebrations children at junior and infant schools in the borough were given teas and entertainments. The Mayor and Mayoress visited each school and presented every child with a souvenir spoon on behalf of the Corporation. They are seen here presenting the Jubilee spoons to boys of St. John's School, West Ealing, and enjoying tea at Drayton Infants School with some of the children.

28.   From the steps of Ealing Town Hall the Town Clerk, Mr R. H. Wanklyn, reads the message to His Majesty King George V from the members of the Boys Brigade for the Silver Jubilee. The silver baton containing the message had originated in Londonderry, and in this picture three boys from 16th (Hanwell) Company, who brought the message from Southall, pass the baton on to boys of 11th (Ealing) Company who were to take it on its next stage to Shepherd's Bush. The baton was handed to The Duke of York at the Albert Hall who in turn handed it on to the King.

29. Southall Market was founded in 1698 by a Charter of William III (see *Environs of Ealing*) and is now one of the last surviving livestock markets in London. The dealers come from as far afield as Bedford and Reading to buy and sell at the market. Horses and ponies now make up the bulk of the livestock on sale. The market has been run by the Steel family since 1870, and this busy scene was photographed in about 1935.

30. In 1906 Ealing Tenants Ltd (see Plate 7) opened their own co-operative grocery and outfitting shop in Pitshanger Lane. This venture proved unsuccessful, but before this there had been only one shop in the lane. The parade shown here in *c*.1935 was built on the north side in 1910 between Barnfield and Lindfield Roads and was known then as Queen's Parade.

31.   A general view taken in September 1935 showing the roundabout on the Western Avenue at the junction with Ealing Road, looking west. The part of Ealing Road on the left was later called Kensington Road. This was a new design in roundabout layout — the first of its kind in the country. A contemporary description states: 'With an ordinary central island, the surrounding road is duplicated on each of the four segments of the circle, so that when in the ordinary course of events shops or public-houses spring into existence on the four corners cars, vans or lorries can draw up in front of them in the secondary road without blocking the fairway for through traffic.'

32.   One of the classrooms in Priory Infants School, Acton Lane *c.*1935. The school opened in 1882 and was one of the first large schools erected in the district, as well as being one of the first to be designed with classrooms surrounding a central hall. This hall was the largest in Acton until the opening of the Public Baths and was used for many years for public meetings. The Board Room of the School Boards and the Education Committee's offices were there until the new Town Hall was completed. In September 1974 it became a First School and closed on 31st August 1981.

33.   One of the familiar landmarks of South Road, the Palace Cinema, was already built in 1936 as this photograph shows. It was opened in November 1929, and is one of the most distinctive of the architect George Cole's cinemas. Built in Chinese style with pagoda pantiled roofs, fierce dragon's head finials and lavish use of coloured faience tiling, it was variously known as the Gaumont, Odeon, Godeon, Godina and then the Liberty. It is now no longer used as a cinema but has been converted into a covered market.

34.   The 14th annual horse parade organized by the
Ealing and District Branch of the R.S.P.C.A. was held on
1st June 1936. Over three hundred horses were entered
and assembled on Ealing Common. From there they
proceeded via The Mall, Ealing Broadway, High Street,
St. Mary's Road and Little Ealing Lane to Northfields
Park where the judging took place. Photographed with
the winner of the Class 1 (Large London Firms) Silver
Cup are the Mayor and Mayoress of Ealing, Alderman
and Mrs J. J. Lynch. On the extreme right is R.S.P.C.A.
Inspector E. P. Kenzie.

(Photo: Mrs Betty Smith)

35.   Southall's Charter Celebrations took place on
24th September 1936, and it was estimated that some ten
thousand people were present in Southall Park when the
Charter was formally handed to Mr W. Garrod, Charter
Mayor. Southall's Charter was one of the few to be
granted during Edward VIII's short reign. Many shops
and buildings were decorated with flags and bunting for
the occasion including the Town Hall.

36. On the accession of King George VI in 1936 the Mayor of Ealing, Councillor F. F. Woodward, read the proclamation from the steps of the Town Hall. He was accompanied by the Mayoress, the Vicar of Ealing (Revd H. Greatbatch) and the Town Clerk (Mr R. H. Wanklyn). A fanfare was played by trumpeters of the Hanwell Silver Band.

37. These houses in Halsbury Road West, Northolt were built on part of Wood End Green Farm and had been newly completed when this view was taken in about 1936. On the right can be seen the estate office. A copy of the sale catalogue makes many claims for these houses. The aim was said to be to give every resident a 'sense of space and freedom from overcrowding', and the houses were offered for £795 freehold. It was claimed that householders here could enjoy the 'rural surrounding of Wood End Green Estate . . . without the disadvantage of isolation from London.'

38. The coronation of King George VI in May 1937 provided another chance for the people of the borough to decorate their streets and shops. The celebrations took many forms — the happy gathering here is a street tea party in Charles Street, Ealing.

39.   St. Matthews Road, Ealing was once more decorated in fine style and even managed to surpass the Silver Jubilee efforts (see Plate 21).

40. The parade of shops on the left between Bond Street and Barnes Pikle was built early in the 1930s, about seven years before this photograph was taken. Trolley bus route 607 had replaced the trams in November 1936, and the Forum Cinema, which can just be seen on the left with the two flagpoles, was opened in April 1934. It was designed by J. Stanley Beard for Herbert A. Yapp and has quasi-Egyptian detailing of black columns set against white faience. In 1961 it became the ABC, and in 1975 it was converted into three small studios. One notable contrast between this view and today's view is the absence of tall office blocks along the Uxbridge Road on the way to West Ealing.

41. Jubilee Park and Jubilee Gardens, Southall were named in commemoration of the Silver Jubilee of King George V and Queen Mary. This crowd is attending the opening ceremony by the Mayor, Alderman G. A. Pargiter, in May 1938. A temporary platform was erected in the roadway near the park gates for the occasion. The complex was intended to meet the needs of North Southall, and included a branch library, health centre, and recreation ground.

42. In 1938 urgent preparations for war were in hand throughout the country. The first public intimation in Ealing that events had taken a grave turn was in September of that year when advice was given from cinema stages that people should go to be fitted with gas masks as soon as possible. As this photograph shows, trenches for use as refuges during air raids were already being constructed in Walpole Park (as they were also in Lammas, Pitshanger, Ravenor, Perivale and Islip Manor Parks, as well as on Ealing Common, Horsenden Hill and Dean Gardens). A thousand men, many of whom were previously unemployed, were engaged day and night on digging the trenches. It was estimated that the trenches, which were bomb proof, except in the case of a direct hit, would accommodate about one-tenth of the population of Ealing.

43. On 1st July 1939 a great National Service recruiting rally was held in Walpole Park when the Rt. Hon. Anthony Eden M.P. was one of the speakers. There was a procession through the town to Walpole Park, and this photograph shows the women's A.R.P. volunteers on parade for the first time when they took part in that procession.

44.   On 1st September 1939 the first party of schoolchildren to be evacuated from West London was marshalled on to Great Western Railway trains at Ealing Broadway. Each child wore a label and carried two packages, one of clothing and the other of food. Approximately fifty thousand children passed through Ealing during the day. The first trains arrived at 7.30 a.m. and they continued until 5.45 p.m., with main line trains arriving every nine minutes. At this time only part of the Borough of Ealing — Ealing and Hanwell south of the Great Western main line — was an evacuation area. Just over three thousand children were sent from there to Hertfordshire, Buckinghamshire, Oxfordshire and Berkshire. In October the evacuation area was extended to include North Ealing, North Hanwell, Greenford and Northolt, and 4,152 children were sent to various places in the Home Counties, West of England and South Wales.

45.   By 1940 appeals were made for all scrap metal, and the people in the borough responded with great enthusiasm. Some of the wide variety of items collected can be seen in this picture.

46. Damage from bombing was scattered over the borough, but in spite of this morale was generally very good. This group are giving the 'thumbs up' from the wreckage of a house in Studland Road, Hanwell after a high explosive bomb fell on 16th September 1940.

47. On 26th September 1940 a high explosive bomb fell on Coldershaw Road. This flat over Jarvis's, grocers, 139 Broadway, West Ealing was among the buildings damaged.

48. One of the buildings totally destroyed was St. Saviour's Church in The Grove, Ealing. Three incendiary bombs fell on the building on 16th November 1940. The clergy and two or three wardens saved what treasures they could, including the vestments and sacred vessels, but the whole of the interior of the church was gutted except for the baptistry and west end.
St. Saviour's was built in 1899 but was not rebuilt after the bombing. The parish joined with the neighbouring Christ Church which became known as the Church of Christ the Saviour.

49. Jones & Knight's store was damaged on 8th December 1940 during intense raids on the London area. Shop assistants are seen here salvaging clothes from the damaged premises. The store closed in the early 1960s and Budgen's supermarket now stands on the site.

50. Southall's War Weapons Week was from 17th to 24th May 1941, when nearly £349,000 was raised. A Grand Procession of 3,000 members of service and ex-service organizations in the borough took place on 18th May. The A.R.P. sections are seen here with a stretcher-party car carrying a seven-foot model of a bomb on the roof. This car had earlier taken part in a parade on Constitution Hill as part of Greater London's War Weapons Week. Southall's car was singled out for special attention and its occupants, Mr W. Haydn Perkins (Chairman of Southall's War Weapons Week Committee), Mr J. L. Bettridge (Deputy Town Clerk) and Mr E. A. Weeks (Publicity Secretary), were introduced to Lord Kindersley (President of the National Savings Committee) and Lord Mottistone (Chairman).

51. The collecting of waste paper was an important part of the war effort, and Southall workers are seen here with some of the salvage collected in September 1941.

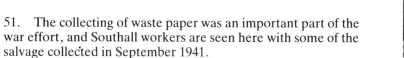

52.   The site for Acton Hospital was provided by the Rothschilds and the building was given by Mr Passmore Edwards, the philanthropic newspaper tycoon, after whom it was named. Lady Rothschild laid the foundation stone in June 1897, and the hospital opened in May of the following year. During the Second World War it was declared an 'Emergency Medical Service Hospital' and was therefore able to take army casualties. This photograph records the visit of Mrs R. A. James, County Commissioner of the Middlesex British Red Cross, on 27th October 1941.

WE MUST ACHIEVE OUR TARGET & PAY FOR — H.M.S.PARTRIDGE

53.   This working party of Greenford women attached to Oldfield Infants School are mending children's clothes for those whose mothers were on war work. The photograph was taken on 19th December 1941 to celebrate the first anniversary of the formation of the group by the headmistress, Miss F. Parkin.

54.   Ealing hoped to raise £700,000 during Warship Week in March 1942 in order to adopt the destroyer HMS *Partridge*. In fact the total collected exceeded this by £70,000, thanks to the hard work of everyone in the borough. A great variety of imaginative fund raising schemes were thought up. The boys of Coston Junior School made a display of 'Greenford Harbour' incorporating a model ship, HMS *Coston*, which had two funnels. The children put their pocket money and other money raised by selling their toys and treasures into these funnels and the total amount collected in this way was £11.3s.4d. HMS *Partridge* was later destroyed by enemy action in January 1943.

55 & 56. Landgirls were a familiar scene in the borough during the war. These two views show them at work in the potato fields in Greenford Road in 1942.

57.   Children of the next of kin of prisoners of war from Ealing were the guests of the British Red Cross at two parties in the Blue Triangle Hall in December 1942. The Mayor of Ealing, Councillor H. G. Greenwood, is seen here with Father Christmas and some of the children. Well over fifty children between the ages of two and seven, and their mothers, were entertained. The hall was lent by the Y.W.C.A., and older children up to fourteen years were entertained the next day at a separate party.

58.   Ealing Wings for Victory Week (6th–13th March 1943) was opened by Air Vice-Marshall F. H. M. Maynard C.B., A.F.C., a son of a former vicar of St. Stephen's, West Ealing. He addressed a parade of Royal Air Force and Civil Defence personnel together with contingents from local organizations in Walpole Park. Members of the A.T.C. and Civil Defence can be seen in the centre and foreground of this assembly which followed the parade.

59.   Ealing's target for Wings for Victory Week was £700,000, but the total borough collection by the end of the week reached the record figure of £1,104,189. Amongst many and varied schemes to raise money was this W.V.S. bomb which had savings stamps to the value of £90 affixed to it and cancelled. It is being displayed here in Dean Gardens, West Ealing, and the lady on the left is Mrs Wilson, District Leader of the W.V.S. The plane in the background is a Hurricane which was on show in Dean Gardens for the week.

60.   The lady in the centre is wielding her shovel with a will to help clear the debris from the now lost Chiswick branch of the North London line, just south of The Vale, Acton, after an air raid in January 1943. The chimney belongs to the Eastman dyeing and cleaning works.

61 & 62. Two scenes in Templeman Road, Hanwell after a high explosive bomb fell on 15th June 1943. In the first a policeman contemplates the damage caused, and in the next a workman rests on his broom for a moment while he watches others clearing the site.

63. In 1865 a Devonshire man, John Sanders, founded the well-known Ealing department store. He started with one shop on the corner of Uxbridge Road and Lancaster Road, and gradually acquired shop after shop on the Broadway. By 1920 he owned two rows of shops, Nos 54–60 and 69–79 The Broadway, together with several other properties in the area. In 1925 he sold the firm to the Rowse brothers, and in late 1932 reconstruction and rebuilding took place to give a single harmonious façade. On 3rd July 1944 a flying bomb caused the damage seen here to the western end of the drapery store. Until 1958 when work started on the new store the bomb damage was hidden by a neatly fenced garden.

64. Another flying bomb on 21st July 1944 caused this damage to shops on the south side of the Uxbridge Road (Nos 197–203), West Ealing.

65. V.E. Day (8th May 1945) gave the people of the borough yet another excuse to decorate their shops and houses. Many street parties reminiscent of the Coronation celebrations in 1937 took place in spite of food rationing. These children from the Brentham Estate are enjoying their party at the corner of Winscombe Crescent, Brunner Road and Woodfield Crescent. Special thanksgiving services took place throughout the borough, and Ealing Green was decorated with red, white and blue fairy lamps. A contemporary report says that many thousands of people danced on The Green until 2 a.m. and that the final dance, to the old Cockney tune of 'Knees Up, Mother Brown', was performed with zest.

66. In 1929 Basil Dean formed a company called Associated Talking Pictures (ATP), and Ealing Green was chosen as the ideal site for the studios which were built in 1931. The official opening by the Duke of Windsor, then Prince of Wales, took place on 3rd March 1932 and just over fourteen years later on 26th June 1946 Princess Elizabeth and Princess Margaret Rose visited the studios. Seen here, with Michael Balcon between them, they made a tour of the studios beginning with a visit to the stage where *Nicholas Nickleby* was being directed by Cavalcanti. Many world famous comedies were made at the studios, which were finally sold to the BBC in 1955.